Cheese, Please!

We climb on the bus.
We all say, "Cheese!"

We run down a hill.
We all say, "Cheese!"

CITY

5

We feed the ducks.
We all say, "Cheese!"

We pick up the leaves.
We all say, "Cheese!"

We ride back to town.
We all say, "Cheese!"

We go out for a pizza.
The man says, "Cheese?"

"Cheese on your pizza?"

"Yes, please!"